FLINT KNIVES

Selected Poems 1973 - 2014

MARTIN K. MANLEY

ISBN 978-1-61468-277-6

The Troy Book Makers
291 River Street
Troy, NY

For Anne

and with gratitude to

Doris Vanderlipp
1924 - 2014

Contents

INTRODUCTION

Martin Kent Manley was born in 1955 in Waltham, Mass., the son of James Manley, a science teacher, and Doris Vanderlipp, a poet and artist. The family moved to Schenectady when Martin was young, and he has lived in Schenectady ever since.

A graduate of Linton High School, Martin spent his working life as a church sexton. From his teenage years onward, he has been active in political movements for peace, human rights and social justice across the world.

He was greatly affected by the CIA-led coup in 1973 that overthrew the democratically elected president of Chile, Salvador Allende. During the reign of terror that followed the coup, Martin was active in the Chile Solidarity Club, which worked to welcome refugees fleeing from the Pinochet dictatorship and to publicize human rights abuses in the once-stable democracy.

Martin also worked to end apartheid in South Africa through the Capital District Coalition Against Racism and Apartheid, to end British rule in the north of Ireland through the James Connolly-Trevor McNulty Irish Republican Club and to support the people of El Salvador through the Schenectady Committee in Solidarity with the People of El Salvador.

In Schenectady, he served on the board of the Home Furnishings Program and was active for years with Schenectady Neighborhood Watch. He has been a dedicated member of peace vigils against the Vietnam War, the bombing of Kosovo and the wars in Iraq and Afghanistan.

Martin has been arrested five times for civil disobedience. The first time was in 1985 as one of the "Albany 10" protesting apartheid. His other arrests in 1985 and 1986 were part of a national campaign of civil disobedience organized by A Pledge of Resistance to oppose the United States government's sponsorship of Contra mercenaries in Nicaragua. After his final guilty plea for a Pledge of Resistance arrest, Martin served four days in the Ulster County Jail. He finally got to see Nicaragua when he volunteered to go there on a church mission trip in 2005.

Only a few friends knew that Martin was writing. His body of work, from which these poems were selected, contains musings on relationships, spiritual matters and nature, as well as the political events of the day. In 1988, he wrote:

Everything I ever was
or wanted to say
I wrote
   here on paper and
   if you want to know me
   please just
      read me
   word by word
for I've told you
who I am
   every way I can.

Anne Neville

1973

1   Struggle!

If you have accepted
   the world
   as it is
you have signed away
   your share
   in tomorrow.
No safety anywhere
   is worth
   that price.

The nation will be ours.
   We have only
   to act.
The right to a footnote
   in history
   is human.
It can never be taken
   only
   sold.

1975

2

We are the
dumb cattle
   of
    America
feedlot
packed
content
fat
ready for
slaughter.

1975

3

The time we have
is short.
Tell other people
when you like them
and take
the hours bright
as they come.
Night is close enough
to us all.

1977

4

Sometimes
what might have been...

Your love was
    so hard
    to hold
as hard as
barbed wire
as hard as
understanding
another
as hard to
find as
a black rose
    and...

        ...felt like
        the night sky
        full of
            stars.

1977

5

Have you ever been insane?
    I have.
    I don't tell anyone
    who knows me well or
    not much at all.

                Anyway
it's just a different kind
        of pain.
Take the visions and
cling to them and
try to understand.
Maybe it will stop.

I know there is
something wrong but
the universe
        inverts
every hour
        and
all the rules are
changed again.
All the rules say
you've lost before
you have begun
and there
        is nothing
                solid
                    anywhere.

Can
    I hold
        on
            to you?
No.
    Well.

Drugged and aimless and afraid
waiting hoping hiding tired
the world shrinks and
everything is slow.

And yet like grass
    I grow again...

        1977

6

    And the truth is
    that all of us
    will take all
    the love we can get.

    We need this
       from each other
          the few do
          who
          care who fight
       the nation's currents
          for the joy
          for the pain
     and because
          honor
    is harder and
    harder to serve in
          America.

1978

7

I was
walking around
and looked
down at my
hand full of
    diamonds
from everywhere
    and you
    were one
       of them.

1978

8

You believe
    in me
believe in me.

If only you could see:
    like glass
    like glass
    splinters
    love will
cause you pain.
No one can ever
give all that anyone
really needs.

We
    just
        try.
We just believe
    as long
    as we can
and then it's time
    to leave
    behind
the shining
    shattered glass
        of love.

9

Held fast
    in
    amber
    ice
no turning back
no turning back
    some choices are
    for   ever
       green trees
       weeping greet
       the day.
Like everyone you
    only look for meaning
    in your life
       always
       ask
always   ask
    if there is
       more
         than this.

(Now
then
do you know
what it is to
    never ever
    give up?)

1978

10

It's a
  thistle
I think of now
  when I think
    of you   so
      beautiful
        among many
      others
          yet like a
        thistle
            painful
                too.

1977

11

Ah yes
    could I say anything bitter about it?
    About
        all the women
        whose minds I couldn't touch
for more
than a few moments
        and the way they slipped
        downstream
        all silvery and glittering
        in and out amongst the
        splashing rocks
        all quick and shining
        and so intent on currents.

I'm slower.
I look back and all around
    a lot.
I'm not
   graceful.

They
dance and weave
gliding through the
   ways of life
with beauty even
in the pain.

1978

12

My life is
   a blunt spear
hurled
   to protest
against
   the wind
against
   tomorrow.

1978

13

The sun sets.
It has done that for
thousands of years.

I see the sky
red from my window
   railroad tracks
   old brick buildings
the sky beyond
   drips blood.

Men have been ruled
   by other men
for thousands of years.
   Fight!
The sky is dripping
   blood.

1979

14   Dust

What
   sifts
   into
your living rooms
   is the dust
from foreign lands
dust that

gently sifts
across your
color
TVs
and you choose
not to see it.

Dust from
foreign
battlefields
softly
settling
across
Time magazines
gunpowder dust
dust from above
mass graves
filled with
the aid of our
munitions
powdered
bone dust
dust from
smashed
homes.
Cassinga dust.

(Written after a 1978 air raid by
South African planes on a
refugee/military camp at Cassinga
in Angola)

1979

15

Look
 everyone
 in the eyes.
There will be
 a story in
 every pair

and some are special
 bright and clear
nothing to conceal
 fires inside
burning phosphorous.

Those
 are the
 people
 to know.

1980

16

I learned a lot
    from you.
You always
made me think
and helped to
define my life.
    Before
there was ore
    found
you taught me steel
and then as
stone against
the blade
    you honed me
    sharp.

Now I'm building
    furnaces.
Watch out for rust!
Watch out for rust!

1980

17   Young and Learning

Before there was
    computer
    radar
    fire control
a gun was fired
    one shot to go
beyond the target
then corrected.
    Aim another
    shot to go
    and
        miss.
A good gunner
always hit
    the third time.

1980

18   Los Gringos

Every
    day of
your life
you are asked
by history
    which side
        are
    you on?
and you
    can't
    even
hear the question.

1981

19

This hurts
    already
    pardon me
while I bleed
    on you.
I fell long ago
    inside
but keep on
    going

so
that is why
I try to tell
you who I am.
　　First Vietnam
　　then Chile
　　　　1973
　　meant the wall
　　and not one step
　　　　farther
　　　　back!

I'm still living
in that year
trying to turn
the clock
around to freedom
time again.

That September death
goes on and on
and never seems
to end.

I'm so tired
I only want
to be a weapon
or a tool
well used.

20   Prayer for New Recruits

O God
    don't send
    us any more
        poets
        no more singers
        no orators
    send some
        executioners
        men who like
        to work
        in dark
        blood spattered
        rooms.

The dreamers
    never last
        and we don't need
        martyrs any longer.

We need to win.

1981

21   Greetings From the Death Squad (El Salvador, 1981)

I want to
    mention empty chairs
        and silent
        hearts
        missing hands
        empty minds
        sightless
            eyes
        and quiet times
and spaces in old
photographs
places in the factory
and office desks
where no one sits today
and all the
empty magazines and
shell casings
spent
burnt powder edged
bullet holes
that filled pledges
side by side
        and all those
        promises
        that went
        with what

                    a life might bring
                    by love directed
                         carefully
          vacant church pews
          untilled fields
          clean coffee cups
          and shorter
          unemployment lines
                    the news
                    of death
                    fills quick
                    dug graves
                    fills the lives
                    of those
                         still left.

1981

22   Memo: State Dept.

The silence
you observe
while killers hunt
your unarmed prey
I curse you for it.
I will that every day
of every year
of every one
of all your lives be
filled with a memory
of screams
of visions of the tears
of all those
who lost as loved
the thousands murdered
while you looked
the other way.

23   Reflections on this Death
(Margaret M. Hess, 1921 - 1981)

Running
   running
      running
         through life
           days
           pass
like hours
   hours like minutes
minutes passing fast
and faster still
recalling all
those you raised
the times
you needed them
   voices laughing
   voices crying
voices trying not
     to weep at
one disappointment
   or another
in some small life beginning.

Understanding
   eludes us
      too well
         sometimes
children growing
still yours but not
quite yours
     anymore
friends and family
voices familiar
voices at the end
were you ever lonely then?

Reaching for
another mind
reaching thirsty
         for
the well of all
   the world
   that's yet unknown.

Woman of another time
woman marked by a
     forgotten war
I salute you
    for
your life lived
as best as you could
     salute you
       for
    what I see
     in your
       daughter's
         eyes.

24   Flint Knives

I.
What stands
    between the two of us
the forceful flow of
    many minds in time
        erases what
        so fine
was in your eyes that
    we had looked
    into each other's
    lives for confirmation
        of
each of our
    own ways to go.

My voice on some
bright copper wire
can speak interminably
    of nothing
and behind
    the sound
I silently
    ask you if
        you care.

If you are there
please look again
for from here
near the
center of myself
I brokenly cry out.

I'm in mourning every day.
   Ghosts are speaking
   at my side
   to keep
memory alive.
I remember everything
      sharp as sharp
        flint knives.

Allende!
died suddenly
fighting still
for what he
   lived for
all his life
   and I remember everything.
My life is one straight line.
I cannot move
   from side to side.

         II.
Something must survive.
Rock needs sand
   to rest on
bird the air to fly
and fishes current going
from mountain down
   to ocean.

III.
Now
let us mourn
all that must
be built
with old bones white
bones to serve
as girders
risers
trestles
and bracings to a "T"
        formation
Facing cold mornings
at dawn the construct
    ing
    workers
fit the sockets to each other
lifting skeletons
        high
    above the dusty
    breeze
    from off the river
    shining in the Sun over fields
    that might
belong to everyone.

IV.
The dead do truly
    understand
what life is all about.
    It's finding out
        how high
the cost of buying
future freedom is

I'm dying by
   degrees
      for the steel clearly
   won't strike
   a single fucking
   spark that holds
a light
   and there's no gasoline.

But when Ignite
   time comes
nothing stops a people
except perhaps that glow
  of military pride
  that mushrooms up a hopeful
  genocidal
      blush across
      victory's veiled face.

1981

25

My
    love
slept uneasy
out of sight
    tangled
    dreams safe soft
       night
          dark
passed to
      day again.

When
we
met
and coming to
know anew
your mind
your life
wakes old
    memories
strong memories
    wakes
      love
        again.

We are
    always
    all alone
with our thoughts

and I'm alone
    with mine.

So
I remember times
    with you
things you'll not
    recall
mattered to me then
as now your recollections
    reveal
what mattered to you
    what I've forgotten
        totally.

So many things
    remind
    me of you
Anytime I see
    a half
        dollar
in a drawer
your photograph
    a tapestry
        a cup
I don't know
what to do with
and the red flag
    waiting
    on the shelf.

What I've
    forgotten
you remember.

What you forgot
I still recall.

It's all the same
everywhere you go
but I want no part
of a life that's dying.

What is real is running
    on the broken
        leg.

        1982

26

House of your
        life
home of your
        love
    inhabited anew.

I refuse ever
    to be kept
    just on the
        front step.

Now I become
    one who
    leaves
    before arriving
    every time
        I see you.

1981

27

My country
I am sorry for you:
    future
    squandered
    past forgotten
you live in the
    hopeful
    eternal
    present.

Your heroes are
not honored not even
when they are dead.
Your leaders
    are criminals
escaped the arms
Justice proffered
    to lie with
    corporations
    instead.

Now you speak of
freedom.   Ah! It's but
a dried out husk
of what the world
once saw. It's all
sucked dry
bones cleaned white
looking for the last
red and blue super-profit.

28   Talisman

Wet night
20th century
roads
towns glow
beyond
the
silhouetted
dark
tree line.

Talisman
I carry
as magic
as memory
as reminder
of
who you
are to
me.

Now
we who
breathe
for gasping
suffocants
see
for groping
blind
walk for
legless many
and heal

the bleeding
mind
plow the sea
willingly
endlessly.

Oh
don't tell
Cassandra
tales
don't tell
any emperor
what ails
his realm
don't expect
anything
but hard
    hard
stones
fast thrown.

What
talisman
faith
dictates
we carry
carefully
along
    carry
talisman along
    singing
bitter songs
of defeat
and sweet
    release.

O
freedom!

Come along
we wait
    each
    with
    talisman
reminder
binder
to the past.

1983

29   Nora Goff Manley
(1899-1982)

Gone
    but
        not
entirely yet
    gone.

After so many
years
a strong will
is like
a berry stain
on the fabric
    of life.

It never
    quite
    fades out.

30   Peace Vigil

You
and you
and you
and you
who see me
from the
corner
of
your
mind's eye
never
realize the
reasons
for what
I do
as my
presence
briefly
flits
across
your vision.

I dance hard
submerged in
spirit world
ghost-like
as if
already
gone
and returned
by force
of will.

By force of will
appear
stand still
wait
stand vigil
for each of you.
I stand vigil
for all
of you.

1985

31

You are
    ocean
    salt
    water
    coelacanth
surface wave
    sky
    clouds
    and
    fish
    concealed.

You are
    ocean
    so
I build
sand castle
walls
    against your
sweeping tide.

You are ocean
    pull me
        under into
all your depths
    as I
        let go.

You are ocean
water mixed
    with blood
blood salt as
    water
inland
    fires
gulls
    sand
stones upon
the shore
where seals
    abide.

You are ocean
    tongue
    of every
sea united
    which I
thirsty
    drink
only to go mad
    from salt
    and sun.

1985

32

She
loves
   me
   as
  much
   or
  more
as
anyone
   ever
   in
her
   life
and always
   has
and always
   will.

When you
   love
     that
      hard
you can't let go
   and
     everything
     hurts
     so
     much

harder
than
it
should.

You
have to know
the other's there
so close you
almost make him
part of you.

Wrenched from
   his life
rails bent on
   fires
strike him over
and over again
for only one
who moves to
   meet you
and shows pain
   can prove
      he cares.

Torn
   apart
and
battered
empty
   inside
you
try
desperately

to
recover
for
a love
    like
    that.

1985

33

Turning
    alone
    into
    pain, pain
        into anger
anger into
    brick wall
    and
    silence
    building
    alone
anew
again.

I remember
    when we
        were kids
one led
        (the best.)
We followed.

        Gang
    chose at times
someone
        who didn't
fit in so well
    to
    leave behind.

Everybody
    ran
        away fast
                away
and someone always got left
suddenly all alone.

Over and over the game was
        played and the skinny
Indian
girl
    was
        chased
                with sticks.

1985

34

Like
   a bank
      with all its
         loans
           out
I've promised away
  more than I have
       to give.
Don't
   everyone
    all
    withdraw
  at
    once
      please.

1985

35   Death Poem

Now
I become
mist
a cobweb against
your cheek
heron call
first flowers

44

in spring
snowflakes
    melt
streams
    barbed
        wire
    rusted
    dew
    diamond like
the word
    against
        the wind
the wind itself
    the word
falling
forever
in night
        trees bare
        before the
           sky
and
    geese
        from North
        aloft
    flying in
    night
        mist
    flying forever
        in
        mist
        in
        night
        toward
        dawn.

1986

36

Wood
metal
tools like
hands
themselves
as I
become
father to
the work.

1986

37

The sure
knowledge of
love
that dances
acrobatic in
the darkening
night air like
firefly
like
magic light
like wings
against fingertips
that come
and go
for I

patient
know
that light
will come around
again
to be caught
in hand
and treasured
 held.

1986

38

I love it
   when you
   let me
   touch you.
I feel
   as though
   I'm past
   the edge
   of what
   I know
and lost
   in the
   mystery
      of
   woman.

1986

39

How sad
I'm in the way
now
you can't
hurt me
too much
get rid
of me
fast enough.

How to
love you
for yourself?
wild and hurt
nurtured by
my love
you healed
to rend me.

How little you
tell yourself
(you still love me)
how little you
know
me
or
yourself.

You must think
I'm weak.

I knew
the path ahead
and where it led
took it
and warned you
every way I could.

And it's not weak
to give and
go on giving
not weak
to need
and go on needing
only weak to give
when the gift is
unwanted.

Yet everything
I saw and said
was true.
When you ceased to see
your perfect image
in my eyes
I ceased to be
for you.

I remember you so
brave before the world
and loved
see now how
afraid of your own self
you are.

Perhaps your instinct is
better than my own and
everything will yet
balance out again
like some great mobile
slowly turning
and I'll
be back where I belong.
But don't count on it.

Why would I
take a chance
on going through
all this again?

1986

40

I look again
at what
I wrote
and still see
the same harsh love
pain
and
tense white vision
focused
see you as if
through a
fog
almost at
the mark of
view
a dark outline form
your destiny contained.

1986

41

This is
    like
going
    room to
    room in
    the empty
    house
    you are
    moving from
and turning off
    the light
    switches
    one
    by
    one.

1986

42

The never ending
   list
things to do
  life just
  slipping away
  just slipping
         away
    never enough
            time
            or
            money
            or
            courage for
            the fight ahead.
    I weep inside
            without
        knowing why
           love
           without
        knowing how.

1986

43

I found
a squirrel
locked in
the steel
toolshed
this morning
cornered
eyes
afraid
scattered sand
outside
to show
how at night
its mate
had tried
to dig it
out.

1986

44

Winter catches
    spring
along the road
    to summer
    and
slaughters her
    with
    ice.

1986

45

What is
    fire
but the
    freed
soul of
    wood
leaping
    joyful?

1986

46   Ollie North

Congress is upset.
A matter of
principle.
The money for
the killing
was sent
before it was approved.

(Lieutenant Colonel Oliver North, an aide to
President Reagan, sold weapons to Iran to
fund the Contras in Nicaragua after Congress
declined to support them.)

1986

47

Many
are
silent.

Those
who
speak

must
speak
louder.

1986

48   Sentry

There is
    more dignity
in one
    lone
    Nicaraguan
    militiaman
        on guard
than in all
    the United States
    Congress
        in session.

49   Party Card

For the comrades of the Comintern
who were murdered by Stalin:

> We work before
> fire
> whose past
> is myth
> and speaks
> to say
> "Trust me
> always."
> and fire is bright
> and fire is strong
> and fire is graceful
> dancing
> but behind the smoke
> of withered years
> are perceived
> whole fields
> whence charred bones
> protrude
> as ready harvest.
>
> (Face to enemy
> they stood.
> The fatal blows
> were from behind.)

(Still loyal
they burn
beneath the earth
forever in
contended fields
watered by
warm spring rains
dripping salty
tears of blood
rivulets in ash.)

1986

50   A Pledge of Resistance

Organized movement
many people
gathering

listening to
last instructions
in the cathedral
entry
ready to march
soon to
try to
block the intersection
a little nervous
and the
loudspeaker
cuts in over
the words

already there
telling others
grouped
be ready
to move
in only
five minutes.

The amplified voice
and that of the woman
before us rise
and fall against
each other
in competition for
our attention.

And I know
we are where
we should be
we are what
we should be
doing what
we should be
doing
together

for peace
together
for justice
together
for honor
and love.
Together we
carry victory
merely by
existing.

(On March 3, 1986, protestors objecting
to the U.S. funding of the Contras in
Nicaragua blocked a main intersection in
Albany, N.Y., and were arrested. After his
fifth civil disobedience arrest on June 26,
1986, this time for refusing to leave the
federal building in Albany, Martin spent
four days in the Ulster County Jail.)

1986

51   Poem Sent From Jail
July, 1986

Love
     you
hold so tight
     don't
you know
I'll never
leave you?

NICARAGUA

My comrades
     die
four days
in jail
are nothing
yet who
understands me
and why
     I am here?

FRIENDS

The love of
friends
forms threads
which find
a way
across hills
trees
over fences
highways
cars
past the coiled
concertina wire
guard desks
through bars
to sing
and speak
with all the voice
of memory contained

so this is easy
alone in this cell
as love
crowds in.

TIME

passes slowly
    for some.

Others here
        they
    are caught
    in this

at ends
of who
they can be.

I'm still at a
    beginning
    still moving
    slowly forward
      toward
       life
        toward
        fate
        toward
           victory.

1987

52

Your life
fell
stone like
into the
waiting pond
of mine
rippled against
the limit
of my shore
and back
again
rippled back
and forth
back and

forth again

My surface
broken I
enclose you
down within
me as durable
as stone
as hard
as stone
as smooth
as stone
as water worn
as stone.

Your surface
whispers of
fire of
weight of
sedimentary lines
of ages of
time elapsed and
you remain
deep inside me
still afire.

1987

53   Geode

Now that
    I'm cracked
       open
    what do you
      find
         inside?

1987

54

Night finally
    quiets by
    exhaustion my
    still unanswered
      questions as
I walk through
    the paper
    tombstones
    cemetery of
whatever it was
    we once were
    to each other.

55   Titanic

Sometimes closing
watertight doors
doesn't help
and the ship
    just
    sinks
    anyway.

The band still playing
fear
screaming
courage
calm
then
drifting off
to sleep
in icy
water
never
to awake.

And
after years and years
the clean
broken wreck
seen alone
proud
every atom of iron
striving for
shore

devoid
of
any human
remains.

Chorus:

We sailed
upon the ocean
dancing in
our ship
we thought
the ocean was
our friend
but then
it turned
on us
and took
us in
interrupting our
busy lives.

1987

56

I have walked
a thousand times
the battlefield
of my own dead
and couldn't ever
bring even one
of them to life
        again.

1987

57

It is
Wednesday
August 5th
7:15 p.m.

I am alone here
in the church
ringing the bell
for Hiroshima.
People passing by
don't know
what I'm doing
    or why.

I am wondering
how long
can a nation
with no conscience
    survive?

1988

58   To a Building

My hand is in
your brush-stroked
paint
and
chiseled into doors
patches in your
broken walls
written in the files
I kept
on everything
I fixed or built.

I was here so
long that I
became a
part of you
proud of
everything I did
my labor
and my love
always will
remain...

1988

59

Our bodies
    our lives themselves
    are but
       levers
    to move the great
    stones of
       history.

Miscalculate and
    everything you are is
    lost   gone
    crushed
       to no avail.

Get it right and
    another stone
    moves slowly
       into place.

1988

60

O friend
don't you know
the Holocaust
is now
everywhere
and in
our name
is in so many places
over and over
again and again
now
and in
our name
the Holocaust
is now
today
    and in
    our name.

1989

61

Chile dies
again
    every day
dies when
anyone plays
    Jara
(who sang
    what
could have been)
dies again
when someone
falls before
the guns
along the wall
he painted
    slogans on.

Chile dies again
when the travel page
runs an item
on ski vacations
in the Andes
dies again
when exiles
home at last
can't join because
they've been away
    too long.

Chile dies again
like Christ
before you
ever unseen
because
A.P. and U.P.I.
never got it
right to begin with
and sure as hell
won't tell it now
for in this
Disney World
of fantasy
we live in
there's no room
for death
or anything
else that's real.

So
Chile dies
on time again
every 11th day
of September
every year
and yet
even dying
even dead and
dying again
and again
Jara songs dying
Allende speeches dying
Neruda poems dying
the ones of the stadium
      dying
the disappeared
      dying
the
      buried Lonquen dead

dying
over and over
again and again.

Even in
her death
Chile lives
and lives braver
and brighter still
lives with flags
higher than ever
    before
lives on in her dead
and all their hopes
and dreams
lives more
alive in death
than these
walking corpses
    here
in the U.S. of A.
    who helped
        to
            kill
                her.

1989

62   Pacific War

Language like
a sand sea
bed bears
the riddled
rusty hulks
of great ideas.

1990

63   Elegy

(John J. Gaffney, 1955-1990)

The great experiment
beckoned us!
Could love be reached
by Northwest Passage
by knowing O
so many strangers' bodies?

Innocent as any child
we played as if there'd be
no tomorrow ever and
now one by one
we discover how

tomorrow arrives
terrible and furious
all covered with sores.

Some of us are good
and some of us are bad.
Some bravely afraid
some nearly insane
with fear.
Some of us are wrapped
in gleaming cloths
of love
and some in
somber cloths of shame.
Some of us have friends
some have none.
Some of us have homes
some are homeless.
Some of us face death alone
and some are held
enough at last
to really matter.

1990

64

Does the tiny
creature trapped
    in amber
mouth awide
    scream
    for all
        eternity?

1990

65

A man
sorts through
a garbage
dumpster. His
kid sits waiting
in a shopping cart
nearby.
What a great
country to provide
these shopping carts
and dumpsters
so the poor
can survive!

1990

66   Explain

How will we
    explain to
    this people
    here
       so well
    dressed having
    everything
       too much
    of everything?

When the day comes
how will we explain
that there is nothing
    left anymore
    after so much
    was taken from
       the land
    and other peoples?

How will we explain
    to this people
    which lives like
    a great spoiled child
    that it's finally
       time to
         pay up?

1991

67   The
Psychology
of the Torpedo

It is launched
it doesn't choose target
or direction
or angle of approach
or speed.
It cannot deviate
from its course.
It lives for
one purpose only.
Success means death.
Failure means death.

1998

68   Depression

O.K. It's
always there
all the time
causeless
formless
if I'm alone
too long
too slow not
busy enough
a hard word

anything
the wave
submerges me
I float for
hours like
minutes in
my own private
ocean
of pain

1999

69

People are a package deal
and everyone's baby has
a few cigarette burns.

What part
of who you are do you wish
to do away with?

Could you give up a leg?
give up your sense of humor?
toss aside an eyeball?
drop some memories down a drain?

You must
you must be better
than you are
be a little
more sane
and
we'll let you know
when you're good enough
to be our friend.

Meanwhile think
about how to be
someone else.
Someone just
like us.

2001

70   Mirror

We are
the Righteous
chosen by
God
to cleanse
the Earth
with Fire
and remake it
in our Image.

2001

71   History

Tell me
America
How was it?
Was it good?
as good
as Wounded Knee?
as good
as Dresden?
as good
as Hiroshima?
or No Gun Ri?
as good as
My Lai or the
Rio Sumpul?
Tell me
America
was it good
for you
too?

2001

72 Flag 1

Washed
a
thousand
times
it
still
runs
blood

2003

73

I respectfully
submit
my wish to be
a bone
in the throat
of Imperialism
hoping to choke
it as it
consumes
before it all
we would have
loved.

74   Thankful For

Blue skies
clouds
honking geese
wheeling down
to water
water flowing
water falling
water still
water frozen.

Iced branches
twigs
in winter light
firelight
wood smoke
leaves aloft
in wind
dancing high
starlight
the full
harvest moon
green grass
crackling
frost
geese honking
over water
water flowing
water falling
water still
frozen earth
spring daffodils.

Thankful for
the word
and the deed
and the dream
and for the memory
of
our dead
who
live on in us.

Thankful for the living.
Thankful for
water falling
water still
water frozen
water flowing.

75   Hiroshima II

What if anyone
even one
of the crew had
said "no"
had then
been replaced
well the
bomb would
still have been
dropped
and the innocent would still
have died
vaporized
or burned
or in slow agony
even decades later
but before
all of history
and God's judgment
of fallible man
there
would have been
at least one
human being
who loved his brothers
enough
to say
"no."

2008

76

José Martí
said that
to be educated
is the only way
to be free
    but
in my country
to be educated
is to be
    a better
       slave.

2008

77   Martin Luther King, Jr.

If we stand on
the shoulders of
giants perhaps
we should not
criticize them.

2008

78

I have
spoken to the deaf
drawn pictures
for the blind
offered food
to those
without tongues
roses for
the rose-less.
Now I
resign myself.
I cannot save
    my country.

2008

79   America

We live in a dream.
The rest of the world
lives in the reality
our dream creates...

2009

80

Given the Christians
available
God must entrust
His work
to sinners.

2011

81

Riding my bicycle
　　into the future
I look back
at everyone else
driving their cars
　　into the past...

2013

82

A thousand years ago
you were working
in a field.
A butterfly
flew up.
Wings brushed
your cheek.
That was me.

2014

83   Safe

I lock my
door at night
to feel safe
but death the
true thief
comes and goes
freely.

2014

84

I'd like it here
on this rock
in the sun
but for the bird
eating my heart.

2014

85

I rode
my bike past
the liquor store.
I could hear the
whiskey bottles
agitated, clinking
crying out
distressed,
"Martin, Martin!
How can you
forsake us
after all
we've done for you?"

2014

86

Hey,
there's still
a nested bird
left to speak
for God.
We'll need a
bulldozer
over here.

(Inspired by Paula Meehan's
"Death of a Field.")

2014

87   Americans

You love your
Empire like
addicts love
the drug
that kills them.
What's it like
to rule the world?
What's it like
slaves to the rich
to rule this world
so beautiful and
given us
from God?

92

What's it like
to kill the fish?
What's it like
to kill the birds?
What's it like
to kill the animals?
What's it like
to kill everyone
who gets in the way?
What's it like
servants of the Empire
to kill the planet and
everything on it?
What's it like
to kill yourselves?

2014

88   On the Fence?

I'll be a
passive observer
to the revolution
you give birth to
by your indifference.

2014

89   Emperor

Let the
windblown rain
be your
monument.

2014

90

Alive is not
the dance floor.
It is to be
yoked to the cause
like a beaten ox.

2014

91   Civil War
(for my brother)

Our father's
father's father
fought for
the Union.
Now we each
walk our own path
to different
revolutions.
If I
looked into
his eyes I'd
see
fallen rebel
flags
broken in
the dust.
Our father's
father's father
fought an Empire
built on slavery.
So do we.

92   Love Poem

Under the August sun
Gavrilo rests
on scythe
before endless fields
of wheat.
Each stalk
awaits
the tender blade's
caress.

Rest easy
Gavrilo
Serbia is free.

Not but once
has all the universe
of stars
turned around
a single man
alone and afraid
with a gun.

(Gavrilo Princip was a Bosnian Serb
who assassinated the Austrian
Archduke Ferdinand in Sarajevo on
June 28, 1914. This was used as a
pretext for Austria-Hungary's
invasion of Serbia, which led to
World War I.)

2014

93

I love
my country
the way a
mother loves
her son
found standing
bloody rock
in hand
over the broken
corpse of his brother.

2014

94

The sunlit surface
a door
between
two worlds
all these
bright fish
seaweed
waving hello
why would
anyone ever
go back into
the hell
above the waves?

95

I was looking for my lost revolution.
　　I think it needs a diaper change.

I was looking for my lost revolution.
　　I had to house train it
　　with a rolled-up newspaper.

I was looking for my lost revolution.
　　The other revolutions
　　picked on it
　　at school today
　　and it
　　　　doesn't want
　　　　　　to go back
　　　　　　　　ever.

I was looking for my lost revolution.
　　The signs said danger
　　keep out but
　　it can't read.

 I was looking for my lost revolution.
　　Did some stranger say
　　I need help
　　to find
　　my lost puppy?

I was looking for my lost revolution.
　　I hope it's in
　　a station house
　　with an ice cream cone.

I was looking for my lost revolution.
    It's having a smoke
        out back.

I was looking for my lost revolution.
    It's getting a
    skull and rose
        tattoo.

I was looking for my lost revolution.
    It's asleep tonight
behind a dumpster.

I was looking for my lost revolution.
    It's in a nursing home
    and can't remember
        its name.

I was looking for my lost revolution.
    I should ask the
    National Security Agency.

I was looking for my lost revolution
    but a drone
    found it first
    and took it out
        with a
            Hellfire
            missile.

2013

96

So
comrades!
Having sought
revolution
as Christians sought
the return of Jesus,
here we are.
Now our
final battles are
diabetes
high blood pressure
heart attack
stroke
and the wheelchair
waits.

2014

97

Wildfires
dark snow
glacial melting
student riots
in Massachusetts
and California
surely the revolution
to save the planet
has begun. But
wait!
Maybe not.
Apparently
they were just
drunken
assholes
having fun.
Oh well, better luck
next time planet.

ACKNOWLEDGEMENTS

Editing this book involved making selections from almost 700 of Martin Manley's poems. Grateful thanks to Anne Neville for indispensable assistance. Thanks also to Willow Partington, Nora Manley and Douglas Rose, each of whom made major contributions of time and talent to this volume.

Doris Vanderlipp